Through The Waves, I Waited

Anika Munir

India | USA | UK

Made with ❤ on the BookLeaf Publishing Platform
www.bookleafpub.in
www.bookleafpub.com

Dedication

For My Dear RIDIW,
TTA

Preface

When I was young, I met you.

You were incredible. Someone who embodied everything
a person should be.

The poems in this book express the way I felt, the events
we shared, and more.

These poems were all written 20 days after you left.

A part of me will never forget. A part of me will always be
waiting.

For you.

44 25' 36" N, 77 49' 47" W

Acknowledgements

Thank you to my amazing friends, family, and loved ones.

The community we build for ourselves is truly the most important thing we can do.

You all got me through this, and I appreciate and love each one of you.

These Days

15/02/21 09/02/22 01/01/23 09/02/24
17/03/21 14/02/22 29/01/23 14/02/24
19/03/21 15/02/22 09/02/23 19/02/24
23/03/21 06/09/22 09/02/23 19/02/24
08/04/21 10/10/22 14/02/23 15/02/24
20/05/21 17/10/22 24/03/23 15/03/24
12/06/21 24/10/22 14/04/23 17/03/24
15/07/21 28/10/22 15/04/23 02/04/24
06/09/21 11/11/22 19/04/23 10/04/24
23/09/21 12/12/22 20/05/23 19/07/24
16/10/21 16/12/22 30/06/23 20/07/24
11/11/21 16/12/22 15/07/23 01/08/24
25/12/21 25/12/22 22/07/23 03/08/24
26/12/22 06/09/23 23/09/24
28/12/22 14/10/23 22/10/24
10/11/23 06/11/24
26/11/23 08/10/24
24/12/23
25/12/23

Finding you

When I first met you,
I felt something unfamiliar,
A sense that this wasn't just another fleeting moment,
Not a three-month fling,
But something deeper, something real.
You made me feel safe,
Like I could trust you with my every thought,
As if you had walked through my struggles,
Lived through the same things I had.
We were different,
Yet shared a understanding,
It was as though I'd been searching for you my whole life,
And when I found you,
You fit perfectly.
You checked every box,
And surpassed every expectation,
Meeting you renewed my faith,
In love, in destiny, in everything.

Sailboats

I never imagined being on one.
It never crossed my mind,
but then I met you.
Now, every time I pass the water,
hear the seagulls call,
watch other boats come in,
all I think about is you.

Purple Shirt

Your father wore it when he met your mother.
You wore it when you met me.
You just knew I was the one.
Now everytime I think about the colour purple.
I think about you.

Uniform

Your uniform,
Green camo, navy blue,
Epaulets gleaming,
Boots shining bright.
You stood tall,
Brown hair with hints of ginger,
And eyes like light brown honey—
Warm, strong, full of resolve.
I always loved seeing you in it.
Who could have known that uniform would play such a
big part in our story?

Telling you I loved you

Saying "I love you" was the easiest part.
You made me feel safe, at peace, like I was home.
I spoke those words,
And felt my walls fall away.
We never stopped saying it.
Even if it was just "ily".
So ily.

Eggs

You made the best eggs in the world.
There was something about the crisp morning air.
They were packed with veggies, protein, and love.
A glass of fresh orange juice and conversation that
flowed effortlessly.
Dancing together in the kitchen while music blasted.
Can you imagine if every morning felt that way?
A morning filled with those eggs and your love.
I could do it for a lifetime.

Gingerbread Contest

I will win.
You will win.
Who will win?
It's my first time trying this.
Learning that icing isn't glue,
realizing I'm still learning the craft.
But every year,
as the Christmas lights fill the streets,
I think of you.
How I'm going to win that contest,
tease you with every step.
Running errands in the snow for extra candy,
watching TikToks to find new tricks
to beat you.
But there was never any real competition.
It was always about doing something with you,
and that's what made me fall in love with you.

Dumpling and Dennison

When the world feels heavy,
And words overflow in every direction,
I find myself thinking of you—
Of the quiet joy in the simple things.
Like bringing you dumplings after a long day,
Or listening, truly listening,
To every word you shared.
Like checking in, just to know you're okay.
Those little moments—
They speak louder than anything else.

The Ball

A red dress, spaghetti straps, and black sparkly heels,
My dark hair caught the light,
You in your blue suit, dark pants, and brown shoes,
We captured the moments, our hearts were so full that
very night.
You looked at me with a love so pure,
Introduced me to all, made me feel secure.
With your hand in mine, you spun me around,
Showing me a love that knows no bounds.
We danced and danced,
You held me close, and I was complete.
In your arms, you could never let me go,
A love like this, more than I'll ever know.

Wedding Guest

I attended many weddings in our time.
As vows were spoken,
I'd imagine my own words to you.
When the mother of the groom spoke of the joy in
gaining another daughter,
I wondered what your parents would say.
When the bride shared the effort she'd put into the day,
I'd think of how long she'd been planning.
So many questions filled my mind,
but I knew, deep down,
I had to wait—
for our time to be right.
To celebrate our love.
But now, will we ever?

Bikes

I hadn't owned one since fifth grade,
but you loved them.
We rode to raise money,
until one day—
the wind was fresh,
and we cycled by the water,
city bikes,
costing us dollars by the minute.
Yet, we laughed—
through the breeze, the cold air,
we kept riding,
kept laughing.
You led the way,
and in that moment,
I fell in love with bikes.

B.C.

You're on the West Coast,
Miles between us for the first time.
Surfing the waves, growing, learning—
Your journey beyond our province's line.
The joy on your face,
A smile I'll never forget.
In my heart, that moment remains,
A memory, no regret.

Wondering

I find myself wondering if you're okay,
Thoughts of you linger, night and day.
I check my phone, hoping for a sign,
Perhaps a text, a word, a line.
I lose myself in the hours, the time zones' chase,
Marking the moments, waiting for your trace.
A world apart, yet you're always near,
In every quiet second, I hold you here.

Airports

There were days I picked you up from the airport.
Other days, I jumped into your arms.
Airports felt magical because they connected you and
me.
But I never imagined there would come a day when I'd
cry in one.
Now, airports haunt me.
I can't imagine going to another one.
But deep down, I know they're the only places that will
ever connect you and me.
Ever again.

Grief

The first time I saw you cry,
The first time I saw you experience loss,
The first time I saw you lose someone,
I held you close.
I never wanted you to feel that pain again.
But little did I know, I'd have to do it again when you let
me go.

Cane Race

Growing old together was always on the bucket list.
A dream we shared in laughter,
Imagining the years ahead, side by side,
With every wrinkle and gray hair a mark of our story.
Having that cane race at 80.
In the beginning, we never questioned it!
80 was part of the game plan, right?
In the beginning, we never questioned it—
The idea of growing old together seemed so simple,
Like an unspoken promise.
We talked about it casually, as though 80 was a
milestone,
A marker on the map of our adventure,
A far-off destination we knew we'd reach together.
80 was always part of the game plan, right?
We had it all figured out, didn't we?
Maybe I will meet you at 80?

We Will Be Okay

We will be okay.
I will be okay.
You will move to a new city,
And I will stay in mine.
Things will change.
Is it time to let go?
But if it's love, won't it find its way back?

Never Letting Go

The truth about you is that I'll never let you go,
You've left a mark on me, a scar I'll always know.
You see the darkness that others can't see,
And know me in a way no one else can trace.
I shared my fears with you, beneath the bridge's,
Dancing in the gazebo by the water,
And as we sat on that old couch, side by side,
You held my heart, no secrets left to hide.

57 Calls & Texts

I couldn't put my phone down.
All I wanted was to call you.
I waited, hoping you'd pick up.
Just pick up.
It didn't feel like it does in the movies,
where the main character eventually moves on.
But I couldn't stop.
I kept calling.
Eventually, the number of rings decreased.
Eventually, it went straight to voicemail.
Eventually, it didn't go through at all.
But I waited.
I am still waiting.

London

London,
I've never been,
But it was your dream to go,
To see new places,
To live the life you'd always wanted,
You were happy,
But did you doubt I'd support you?
If one can manage three years,
What's one more year?

Tools

Screwdrivers,
Hammers,
Nails,
You'd craft stools,
You'd build shelves,
You built me a dream,
A future,
Of us together,
So why is there no compound to seal the distance
between us?
How can you fix everything else,
But leave us, like this?

Lego

Flowers fade,
But our love can't die.
Right?
I don't want the real ones,
You get me LEGO flower sets instead,
Those will never wither,
They'll forever stay alive,
Unless someone breaks them,
Or parts go missing.
But even then, they'd survive.

Dark Lipstick

My dark lips,
Always maroon,
At times red,
And occasionally pink.

In the Silence

When you left,
They screamed, "His loss."
They said, "He'll come back."
They assured, "You'll be okay."
They promised, "It will take time."
I don't know if they're right.
They claim it's his loss,
But my heart tells a different story.
They say you'll return,
But the unread messages speak otherwise.
They insist I'll heal,
But my eyes show differently,
They tell me time will ease the pain,
But the clock seems to slow down,
It's as if I'm frozen,
Caught in the echoes of your words,
Desperately searching for any sign
That there might still be a future for us.

In Every Scenario

I believe I will always love you.
Even though you're gone,
Sometimes we meet people who leave a mark,
You were that person for me.
Maybe you were my first love,
Maybe you were the hardest love,
Maybe you were the one I was meant to be with.
But in every version,
I saw a lifetime with you.

My Version of SATC

I am not Samantha,
Nor Miranda,
Nor Charlotte,
Nor Carrie,
I am all of them.
I loved you like Charlotte does,
I approached my career and our finances like Miranda,
I was wild with passion like Samantha,
And now, like Carrie, I sit here tonight, writing about
you.

Train Stations

The infamous train,
I walk toward it,
Seeking solitude to reflect on us,
To think about what happened between us.
At times, I pace the platform,
Back and forth, waiting,
Just listening to our song.
Other times, I sit in the station halls,
Where I once use to drop you off,
Passing men with their luggage,
And wonder where you are now,
In this world, carrying yours.

Your Community

Your friends,
Your community,
They cared deeply for you,
And they cared for me too.
We'd spend all night playing board games,
Head to trivia nights,
Stroll through cities,
Grab a drink.
They thought the world of me,
Because you did.
I wonder what they think of me now?
Your community felt like mine,
But deep down, it was always yours.
I wish I could be a part of it,
Even when I am not a part of yours.

Writing All Night

I can't stop writing,
Finding peace in these words,
Finding peace in thoughts of you,
Finding peace in memories of you.
All I can think about is you.
My fingers move quickly,
The laptop I once used to FaceTime you,
Now holds the words of the memories of those calls,
The love we shared.
These words are not meant to hurt,
But to show you that I loved you,
And still do.
I made a promise,
And I kept it.
I am feeling everything,
As I write these words.

If You Had Asked Me

Did I choose this city?
Did I choose these buildings?
Did I choose these trains?
Did I choose these streets?
Did I choose these roads?
Did I choose these restaurants?
Did I choose these parks?
Did I choose these homes?
Did I choose these hospitals?
Did I choose these malls?
Did I choose these highways?
Did I choose these plazas?
Did I choose these statues?
Did I choose these lights?
Did I choose all of this over you?
No, because if you had asked me,
Just once,
I would have chosen you.

Elections

Politics,

The red,

The blue,

But where are you?

Your views shaped by history,

By policy,

We go back and forth,

On the same page,

Always in sync,

As announcements unfold,

Politicians make promises,

But it's your commentary I'll keep in mind.

The Map

There sits a large map
inside my hunter rainboot,
still rolled up,
a gift from you,
from some time ago.
I used to imagine we'd hang it up
once we lived under the same roof,
or that I'd find more space for it.
I always tuck away the postcards,
the paintings,
the rocks I've collected,
all in one box.
Every souvenir you got me.
Every wall, every shelf in this room
is filled with memories of you.
But that map,
it remains unmoved,
a reflection of how our decision to move,
the shifting coordinates,
came to a standstill.

All That Is Left

I thought if I moved,
I would miss the buildings,
miss the familiar streets,
miss the laughter of friends,
miss out on all the stories.
But the truth, as I sit alone,
in this quiet room,
is that all I miss is you.
I thought if I moved,
I would have to start over,
but in truth,
a life without you
is the real restart.
The future I imagined,
so planned,
the dreams I once held dear,
they all had you in them.
I thought moving meant giving them up,
but in reality,
it's those dreams I've lost
for they were all tied to you.
Now, I wish I moved.

Always Will

It will always lead back to you.
You will always be my beginning,
Though I wish you could be my end.
Even when I will reach the finish line,
My thoughts will drift to where it all began—
You.

Hope In My Bones

In my bones, I carry a hope for us,
Though I am aching,
Lost in the void of your absence,
Yet something within my body whispers that this isn't
the end.
But what if it is?
What if all I'm seeing are delusions?
What if this is just a fleeting cure,
A false remedy for the pain I am facing?

Your Stuff

I never truly understood what it meant to be haunted by
someone alive,
But as I sit here in this empty space,
I now know what that feels like.
You might be out at some bar,
Yet your presence lingers within these walls,
Your sweater,
Your photos,
Your books—
All of it haunts me,
While you continue to live without me.

The City

They say the name,
They claim it's where they're from,
And all my mind can think of is you.
They mention they're visiting it,
And I can only think of you.
They speak of news from there,
And my thoughts will always return to that city.
The memories of that place will forever live in my heart.
All because you are there.

I Will Wait

I waited years for you,
For the time to pass,
And in the quiet moments, when I'm alone,
A part of me still waits.
Waiting for you.
Waiting for us.
Because deep down, no matter what,
I still believe we are something.
So I will wait.
Not just for a return,
but for the promise we made,
even when the world moves on,
And the years blur into the past,
I'll hold onto the belief
That we are more than time,
More than distance,
More than anything that could keep us apart.
I'll wait.